JESUS, I TRUST IN YOU!

JESUS, I TRUST IN YOU!

Selected prayers of Saint Faustina

3rd edition

The Shrine of the Divine Mercy
Kraków 1995

Nihil Obstat:
Rev. Tomasz Chmura
Kraków, July 25, 1994

Imprimatur:
Franciszek Cardinal Macharski
Archbishop of Kraków
The Metropolitan Curia
Kraków, August 1, 1994

Printed in the U.S.A. by Pauline Books & Media, 50 Saint
Pauls Avenue, Boston MA 02130-3491.

www.pauline.org

Pauline Books & Media is the publishing house of the
Daughters of St. Paul, an international congregation of
women religious serving the Church with the communica-
tions media.

3 4 5 6 7   05 04 03 02 01

The Church must consider it one of her principal duties—at every stage of history and especially in our modern age—to proclaim and to introduce into life the mystery of mercy, supremely revealed in Jesus Christ. Not only for the Church herself as the community of believers but also in a certain sense for all humanity, this mystery is the source of a life different from the life which can be built by man, who is exposed to the oppressive forces of the threefold concupiscence active within him....

The Church proclaims the truth of God's mercy revealed in the crucified and Risen Christ, and she professes it in various ways. Furthermore, she seeks to practise mercy towards people through people, and she sees in this an indispensable condition for solicitude for a better and "more human" world, today and tomorrow. However, at no time and in no historical period—especially at a moment as critical as our own—can the Church forget the prayer that is a cry for the mercy of God amid the many forms of evil which weigh upon humanity and threaten it. Precisely this is the fundamental right and duty of the Church in Christ Jesus, her right and duty towards God and towards humanity.

John Paul II

(Dives in Misericordia 14.15)

TABLE OF CONTENTS

IV. Selected Prayers from Saint Faustina's Diary

V. Prayer to Obtain Graces through the intercession of Saint Faustina   69

SAINT FAUSTINA

The task of "proclaiming and introducing into life" the mystery of God's mercy, and imploring that mercy for the world, which the Holy Father, Pope John Paul II places before the entire Church, was entrusted to Saint Faustina as her life's witness and mission.

Sister Faustina was born in 1905 in the village of Głogowiec near Łódź as the third of ten children in the family of Marianna and Stanisław Kowalski. From her childhood she was distinguished by a love for prayer, diligence at work, obedience and a sensitivity for the poor. She attended not quite three years of elementary schooling, and later, as a teenager, left her family home to work as a domestic servant.

At the age of twenty she entered the Congregation of the Sisters of Our Lady of Mercy in which, as Sister Maria Faustina, she spent thirteen years of her life performing the duties of cook, gardener, and doorkeeper. Her life, though seemingly very ordinary, monotonous and drab, concealed in itself an exceptionally profound union with God. From her childhood she desired to become a great saint, and she consistently strove toward that goal, working together with Jesus for the salvation of lost souls, even to the extent of offering her life as a sacrifice for sinners. Therefore, her life as a religious was marked with the stigma of suffering, but also with extraordinary mystical graces.

It was to this religious, who though simple, had boundless trust in God, that Jesus directed that amazing declaration, *In the Old Covenant I sent prophets wielding thunderbolts to My people. Today I am sending you with My mercy to the people of the whole world. I do not want to punish aching mankind, but I desire to heal it, pressing it to My Merciful Heart* (1588*).

The mission of Saint Faustina consists in:

—reminding the world of the truth of our faith revealed in Holy Scripture about the merciful love of God towards every human being, even the greatest sinner;

—conveying new forms of devotion to Divine Mercy and

—initiating a great movement of devotees and apostles of Divine Mercy who would lead

---

* The numbers shown in brackets after each quote refer to passages in Saint Faustina's *Diary*.

people toward the renewal of Christian life in the spirit of this devotion; in other words, in the evangelical spirit of a childlike confidence in God and an active love of neighbor.

Worn out and weakened by tuberculosis and the sufferings she bore in sacrifice for sinners, Sister Faustina died in the odor of sanctity in Kraków on October 5, 1938 at the age of 33.

On the first Sunday after Easter, April 18, 1993, in St. Peter's Square in Rome, Pope John Paul II declared her one of the community of the blessed. On the following day during his general audience he said, "God has spoken to us through the spiritual wealth of Blessed Sister Faustina Kowalska. She left to the world the great message of Divine Mercy and an incentive to complete self-surrender to the Creator. God endowed her with a singular grace that enabled her to experience His mercy through mystical encounter and by a special gift of contemplative prayer.

Blessed Sister Faustina, thank you for reminding the world of that great mystery of Divine Mercy; that 'startling mystery,' that inexpressible mystery of the Father, which today every individual and the whole world need so very much."

THE DEVOTION TO THE DIVINE MERCY

according to the forms given to

Saint Faustina

Pope John Paul II
canonized Saint Faustina in Rome
on April 30, 2000.

THE ESSENCE
OF THE
DIVINE MERCY DEVOTION

1. Trust expresses the disposition we should have toward God. It includes not only the virtue of hope, but also a lively faith, humility, perseverance and remorse for sins committed. It is simply the attitude of a child who trusts boundlessly in the merciful love and omnipotence of the Heavenly Father in every situation.

Trust is so essential to the Divine Mercy devotion that without it the devotion cannot exist; this is because our worship of the Divine Mercy is first and foremost an expression of trust. An attitude of trust alone (even without the practice of other forms of the devotion) already assures the trusting soul of grace that it will receive God's mercy. *I desire,* Jesus promised, *to grant unimaginable graces to those souls who trust in My mercy* (687). *Let them approach this sea of mercy with great trust. Sinners will attain justification, and the just will be confirmed in good. Whoever places his trust in My mercy will be filled with My divine peace at the hour of death* (1520).

Trust is not only the essence or soul of this devotion, but also the condition for obtaining graces. *The graces of My mercy,* Jesus told Sister Faustina, *are drawn by means of one vessel only, and that is—trust. The more a soul trusts, the more it will receive. Souls that trust boundlessly are a great comfort to Me, because I pour all the treasures of My graces into them. I rejoice that they ask for much, because it is my desire to give much, very much* (1578). *The soul which will trust in My mercy is most fortunate, because I Myself take care of it* (1273). *No soul that has called upon My mercy has been disappointed or brought to shame. I delight particularly in a soul which has placed its trust in My goodness* (1541).

2. Mercy expresses the disposition we should have towards every human being. Jesus told Sister Faustina, *I demand . . . deeds of mercy, which are to arise out of love for Me. You are to show mercy to your neighbors always and everywhere. You must not shrink from this or try to excuse or absolve yourself from it. I am giving you three ways of exercising* *mercy toward your neighbor: the first–by deed, the second–by word, the third–by prayer. In these three degrees is contained the fullness of mercy and it is an unquestionable proof of love for Me. By this means a soul glorifies and pays reverence to My mercy* (742).

This attitude of an active love of neighbor is also a condition for obtaining graces. Jesus recalled the Gospel maxim when He said, *If a soul does not exercise mercy somehow or other, it will not obtain My mercy on the day of judgement. Oh, if only souls knew how to gather eternal treasure for themselves, they would not be judged, for they would forestall My judgement with their mercy* (1317).

The Lord desires that those who worship Him perform at least one act of mercy every day. *My daughter,* Jesus told Sister Faustina, *know that My Heart is mercy itself. From this sea of mercy, graces flow out upon the whole world. . . . I desire that your heart be an abiding place of My mercy. I desire that this mercy flow out upon the whole world through your heart. Let no one who approaches you go away without that trust in My mercy which I so ardently desire for souls* (1777).

THE IMAGE
OF THE
DIVINE MERCY

The image of the Divine Mercy originates from a vision that Sister Faustina had in Płock on February 22, 1931. In that vision Christ expressed His desire to have such an image painted and that the words in the signature beneath it be: Jesus, I trust in You.

The image represents the risen Christ, whose hands and feet bear the marks of the crucifixion. From His pierced Heart, not visible in the image, two rays issue forth: red and pale. When asked about their meaning Jesus explained, *the pale ray stands for the Water which makes souls righteous. The red ray stands for the Blood which is the life of souls. These two rays issued forth from the very depths of My tender mercy when My agonized Heart was opened by a lance on the Cross* (299). In other words, these two rays signify the Sacraments, and also the Holy Church born of the pierced side of Christ, as well as the gifts of the Holy Spirit, of which water is a symbol in Scripture. *Happy is the one who will dwell in their shelter,* said Jesus, *for the just hand of God shall not lay hold of him* (299).

The image then, portrays the great mercy of God, which was fully revealed in the Paschal Mystery of Christ, and is manifested in the Church most effectively through the Holy Sacraments. The purpose of this image is to serve as a vessel for obtaining graces, and to be a sign which is to remind the world of the need to trust in God and to show mercy toward our neighbor. The words found in the signature beneath the image, *Jesus, I trust in You,* speak of an attitude of trust. The image, Jesus said, *is to be a reminder of the demands of My mercy, because even the strongest faith is of no avail without works* (742).

The veneration of this image is based on confident prayer joined with deeds of mercy. Jesus attached the following promises to the veneration of the image thus understood: the grace of salvation, great progress on the road to Christian perfection, the grace of a happy death, and all other graces and temporal blessings which people who practice mercy will ask Him for with trust.

I am offering people a vessel, Jesus told Sister Faustina, *with which they are to keep coming for graces to the fountain of mercy. That vessel is this image with the signature: ~Jesus, I trust in You~* (327). *By means of this image I shall be granting many graces to souls; so let every soul have access to it* (570). *I promise that the soul that will venerate this image will not perish. I also promise victory over (its) enemies already here on earth, especially at the hour of death. I Myself will defend it as My own glory* (48).

The flames of mercy are burning Me. I desire to pour them out upon human souls. Oh, what pain they cause Me when they do not want to accept them! . . . Tell aching mankind to snuggle close to My merciful Heart, and I will fill it with peace (1074). *Mankind will not have peace until it turns with trust to My mercy* (300).

Speak to the world about My mercy; let all mankind recognize My unfathomable mercy. It is a sign for the end times; after it will come the day of justice. While there is still time, let them have recourse to the fount of My mercy; let them profit from the Blood and Water which gushed forth for them (848). *Before I come as a just Judge, I first open wide the doors of My mercy. He who refuses to pass through the doors of My mercy must pass through the doors of My justice* (1146).

Act of Entrustment to The Divine Mercy

O Most Merciful Jesus, Your goodness is infinite, and the treasures of Your grace inexhaustible. I trust boundlessly in Your mercy, which is above all Your works. I consecrate myself to You completely and unreservedly, so as to live and strive for Christian perfection.

I want to spread Your mercy by performing works of mercy, both spiritual and corporal, laboring especially for the conversion of sinners, bringing consolation to those in need, to the sick and the suffering.

Guard me then, O Jesus, as Your own possession and Your own glory. Though I sometimes tremble with fear, aware of my weakness, at the same time I have boundless trust in Your mercy. Oh, that all people would come to know the infinite depths of Your mercy, while there is still time, so that they may place their trust in Your merciful love and glorify You forever. Amen.

THE FEAST
OF DIVINE MERCY

According to Jesus' wish, the Feast of Mercy is to be celebrated on the first Sunday after Easter. Jesus is showing us the close connection between the Easter mystery of man's Redemption and this feast. The liturgy for this day extols God most fully in the mystery of His mercy.

The Feast of Mercy is to be not only a day designated for the singular worship of God's Mercy , but also a day of grace for all people, particularly for sinners. Jesus attached great promises to this feast, the greatest of which is connected with the reception of Holy Communion on that day. It is the promise of *complete forgiveness of sins and punishment.* In other words, this grace is equal only to the one we receive in the Sacrament of Holy Baptism. The greatness of this feast lies also in the fact that everyone, even those who are converted that very day, may obtain any grace for the asking, if what they ask for be compatible with God's will. *I want this image,* Jesus told Sister Faustina, . . . *to be solemnly blessed on the first Sunday after Easter; that Sunday is to be the Feast of Mercy* (49). *I desire that the Feast of Mercy be a refuge and shelter for all souls, and especially for poor sinners. On that day the very depths of My tender mercy are open. I pour out a whole ocean of graces upon those souls who approach the fount of My mercy. The soul that will go to Confession and receive Holy Communion shall obtain complete forgiveness of sins and punishment. On that day are open all the divine floodgates through which graces flow. Let no soul fear to draw near to Me, even though its sins be as scarlet* (699).

The Feast of My Mercy has issued forth from My very depths for the consolation of the whole world (1517) *and is confirmed in the vast depths of My tender mercies* (420).

The preparation for this feast is to be a novena consisting of the recitation of the Divine Mercy Chaplet for nine days, beginning on Good Friday. Sister Faustina's Diary also contains another novena which Jesus dictated for her own personal use and attached to it a promise regarding her person alone. All Christians may likewise make this novena with fervor and that is why we have included it in this prayer book.

Novena
before the Feast of Mercy

I desire, Jesus told Sister Faustina, *that during these nine days you bring souls to the fount of My mercy, that they may draw therefrom strength and refreshment and whatever graces they need in the hardships of life and, especially, at the hour of death. On each day you will bring to My Heart a different group of souls, and you will immerse them in this ocean of My mercy, and I will bring all these souls into the house of My Father. . . . On each day you will beg My Father, on the strength of My bitter Passion, for graces for these souls.*

First Day

Today, bring to Me all mankind, especially all sinners, and immerse them in the ocean of

My mercy. In this way you will console Me in the bitter grief into which the loss of souls plunges Me.

Most Merciful Jesus, whose very nature it is to have compassion on us and to forgive us, do not look upon our sins, but upon the trust which we place in Your infinite goodness. Receive us all into the abode of Your Most Compassionate Heart, and never let us escape from It. We beg this of You by Your love which unites You to the Father and the Holy Spirit.

Eternal Father, turn Your merciful gaze upon all mankind and especially upon poor sinners, all enfolded in the Most Compassionate Heart of Jesus. For the sake of His sorrowful Passion, show us Your mercy, that we may praise the omnipotence of Your mercy forever and ever. Amen.

The Chaplet of Divine Mercy

Second Day

Today bring to Me the souls of priests and religious, and immerse them in My unfathomable mercy. It was they who gave Me the strength to endure My bitter Passion. Through them, as through channels, My mercy flows out upon mankind.

Most Merciful Jesus, from whom comes all that is good, increase Your grace in us, that we may perform worthy works of mercy, and that all who see us may glorify the Father of Mercy who is in heaven.

Eternal Father, turn Your merciful gaze upon the company (of chosen ones) in Your vineyard–upon the souls of priests and religious; and endow them with the strength of Your blessing. For the love of the Heart of Your Son, in which they are enfolded, impart to them Your power and light, that they may be able to guide others in the way of salvation, and with one voice sing praise to Your bound-less mercy for ages without end. Amen.

The Chaplet of Divine Mercy

Third Day

Today bring to Me all devout and faithful souls, and immerse them in the ocean of My mercy. These souls brought Me consolation on the Way of the Cross. They were that drop of consolation in the midst of an ocean of bitterness.

Most Merciful Jesus, from the treasury of Your mercy, You impart Your graces in great abundance to each and all. Receive us into the abode of Your Most Compassionate Heart and never let us escape from It. We beg this of You by that most wondrous love for the heavenly Father with which Your Heart burns so fiercely.

Eternal Father, turn Your merciful gaze upon faithful souls, as upon the inheritance of Your Son. For the sake of His sorrowful

Passion, grant them Your blessing and surround them with Your constant protection. Thus may they never fail in love or lose the treasure of the holy faith, but rather, with all the hosts of Angels and Saints, may they glorify Your boundless mercy for endless ages. Amen.

The Chaplet of Divine Mercy

Fourth Day

Today bring to Me the pagans and those who do not yet know me. I was thinking also of them during My bitter Passion, and their future zeal comforted My Heart. Immerse them in the ocean of My mercy.

Most Compassionate Jesus, You are the Light of the whole world. Receive into the abode of Your Most Compassionate Heart the souls of pagans who as yet do not know You. Let the rays of Your grace enlighten them that they, too, together with us, may extol Your wonderful mercy; and do not let them escape from the abode which is Your Most Compassionate Heart.

Eternal Father, turn Your merciful gaze upon the souls of pagans and of those who as yet do not know You, but who are enclosed in the Most Compassionate Heart of Jesus. Draw them to the light of the Gospel. These souls do not know what great happiness it is to love You. Grant that they, too, may extol the generosity of Your mercy for endless ages. Amen.

The Chaplet of Divine Mercy

Fifth Day

Today bring to Me the souls of heretics and schismatics, and immerse them in the ocean of My mercy. During My bitter Passion they tore at My Body and Heart; that is, My Church. As they return to unity with the Church, My wounds heal, and in this way they alleviate My Passion.

Most Merciful Jesus, Goodness Itself, You do not refuse light to those who seek it of You. Receive into the abode of Your Most Compassionate Heart the souls of heretics and schismatics. Draw them by Your light into the unity of the Church, and do not let them escape from the abode of Your Most Compassionate Heart; but bring it about that they, too, come to adore the generosity of Your mercy.

Eternal Father, turn Your merciful gaze upon the souls of heretics and schismatics, who have squandered Your blessings and misused Your graces by obstinately persisting in their errors. Do not look upon their errors, but upon the love of Your own Son and upon His bitter Passion, which He underwent for their sake, since they, too, are enclosed in the Most Compassionate Heart of Jesus. Bring it about that they also may glorify Your great mercy for endless ages. Amen.

The Chaplet of Divine Mercy

Sixth Day

Today bring to Me the meek and humble souls and the souls of little children, and immerse them in My mercy. These souls most closely resemble My Heart. They strengthened Me during My bitter agony. I saw them as earthly Angels, who would keep vigil at My altars. I pour out upon them whole torrents of grace. Only the humble soul is able to receive My grace. I favor humble souls with My confidence.

Most Merciful Jesus, You Yourself have said, "Learn from Me for I am meek and humble of heart." Receive into the abode of Your Most Compassionate Heart all meek and humble souls and the souls of little children. These souls send all heaven into ecstasy, and they are the heavenly Father's favorites. They are a sweet-smelling bouquet before the throne of God; God Himself takes delight in their fragrance.

These souls have a permanent abode in Your Most Compassionate Heart, O Jesus, and they unceasingly sing out a hymn of love and mercy.

Eternal Father, turn Your merciful gaze upon meek and humble souls, and upon the souls of little children, who are enfolded in the abode which is the Most Compassionate Heart of Jesus. These souls bear the closest resemblance to Your Son. Their fragrance rises from the earth and reaches Your very throne. Father of mercy and of all goodness, I beg You by the love You bear these souls and by the delight You take in them: bless the whole world, that all souls together may sing out the praises of Your mercy for endless ages. Amen.

The Chaplet of Divine Mercy

Seventh Day

Today bring to Me the souls who especially venerate and glorify My mercy, and immerse them in My mercy. These souls sorrowed most over My Passion and entered most deeply into My Spirit. They are living images of My Compassionate Heart. These souls will shine with a special brightness in the next life. Not one of them will go into the fire of hell. I shall particularly defend each one of them at the hour of death.

Most Merciful Jesus, whose Heart is Love Itself, receive into the abode of Your Most Compassionate Heart the souls of those who particularly extol and venerate the greatness of Your mercy. These souls are mighty with the very power of God Himself. In the midst of all afflictions and adversities they go forward, confident of Your mercy. These souls are united to Jesus and carry all mankind on their shoulders. These souls will not be judged severely, but Your mercy will embrace them as they depart from this life.

Eternal Father, turn Your merciful gaze upon the souls who glorify and venerate Your greatest attribute, that of Your fathomless mercy, and who are enclosed in the Most

Compassionate Heart of Jesus. These souls are a living Gospel; their hands are full of deeds of mercy, and their spirit, overflowing with joy, sings a canticle of mercy to You, O Most High! I beg You O God: Show them Your mercy according to the hope and trust they have placed in You. Let there be accomplished in them the promise of Jesus, who said to them, I Myself will defend as My own glory, during their lifetime, and especially at the hour of their death, those souls who will venerate My fathomless mercy.

The Chaplet of Divine Mercy

Eighth Day

Today bring to Me the souls who are in the prison of Purgatory, and immerse them in the abyss of My mercy. Let the torrents of My Blood cool down their scorching flames. All these souls are greatly loved by Me. They are making retribution to My justice. It is in your power to bring them relief. Draw all the indulgences from the treasury of My Church and offer them the alms of the spirit and pay off their debt to My justice.

Most Merciful Jesus, You Yourself have said that You desire mercy; so I bring into the abode of Your Most Compassionate Heart the souls in Purgatory, souls who are very dear to You, and yet, who must make retribution to Your justice. May the streams of Blood and Water which gushed forth from Your Heart put out the flames of the purifying fire, that in that place, too, the power of Your mercy may be praised.

Eternal Father, turn Your merciful gaze upon the souls suffering in Purgatory, who are enfolded in the Most Compassionate Heart of Jesus. I beg You, by the sorrowful Passion of Jesus Your Son, and by all the bitterness with which His most sacred Soul was flooded, manifest Your mercy to the souls who are under Your just scrutiny. Look upon them in no other way than through the Wounds of Jesus, Your dearly beloved Son; for we firmly believe that there is no limit to Your goodness and compassion.

The Chaplet of Divine Mercy

Ninth Day

Today bring to Me souls who have become lukewarm, and immerse them in the abyss of My mercy. These souls wound My Heart most painfully. My soul suffered the most dreadful loathing in the Garden of Olives because of lukewarm souls. They were the reason I cried out: "Father, take this cup away from Me, if it be Your will." For them, the last hope of salvation is to flee to My mercy.

Most compassionate Jesus, You are Compassion Itself. I bring lukewarm souls into the abode of Your Most Compassionate Heart. In this fire of Your pure love let these tepid souls, who, like corpses, filled You with such deep loathing, be once again set aflame. O Most Compassionate Jesus, exercise the omnipotence of Your mercy and draw them into the very ardor of Your love; and bestow upon them the gift of holy love, for nothing is beyond Your power.

Eternal Father, turn Your merciful gaze upon lukewarm souls, who are nonetheless enfolded in the Most Compassionate Heart of Jesus. Father of Mercy, I beg You by the bitter Passion of Your son and by His three-hour agony on the Cross: Let them, too, glorify the abyss of Your mercy. . . (1209-1229).

The Chaplet of Divine Mercy

Celebrating the Feast of Mercy

It is Jesus' express desire that the image of Divine Mercy be solemnly blessed and given public, (meaning liturgical) veneration, so that priests may tell souls of this great and unfathomable mercy of God.

In order for people to benefit from these great gifts which the Lord wishes to give to every person and all humanity, they should be in the state of grace (i.e., having made a good Holy Confession); they should fulfill the conditions of the Divine Mercy devotion (that of trust and active love of neighbor) and on that day approach the *Source of Life*; in other words, receive Holy Communion.

The Sacrament of Reconciliation and Penance

Jesus' words to Sister Faustina

When you go to Confession, to this fountain of My mercy, the Blood and Water which came forth from My Heart always flow down upon your soul and ennoble it. Every time you go to Confession, immerse yourself entirely in My mercy, with great trust, so that I may pour the bounty of My grace upon your soul. When you approach the confessional, know this, that I Myself am waiting there for you. I am only hidden by the priest, but I Myself act in your soul. Here the misery of the soul meets the God of mercy. Tell souls that from this fount of mercy souls draw graces solely with the vessel of trust. If their trust is great, there is no limit to My generosity. The torrents of grace inundate humble souls. The proud remain always in poverty and misery, because My grace turns away from them to humble souls (1602).

Tell souls where they are to look for solace; that is, in the Tribunal of Mercy. There the greatest miracles take place (and) are incessantly repeated. To avail oneself of this miracle, it is not necessary to go on a great pilgrimage or to carry out some external ceremony; it suffices to come with faith to the feet of My representative and to reveal to him one's misery and the miracle of Divine Mercy will be fully demonstrated. Were a soul like a decaying corpse so that from a human standpoint, there would be no (hope of) restoration and everything would already be lost, it is not so with God. The miracle of Divine Mercy restores that soul in full. Oh, how miserable are those who do not take advantage of the miracle of God's mercy! You will call out in vain, but it will be too late (1448).

Holy Communion

The graces Our Lord has prepared for the Feast of Mercy are connected with full participation in Holy Mass. This includes receiving Holy Communion, to which the promise of *complete forgiveness of sins and punishment* is attached.

Jesus' words to Sister Faustina

I desire to unite Myself with human souls. . . When I come to a human heart in Holy Communion, My hands are full of all kinds of graces which I want to give to the soul. But souls do not even pay any attention to Me; they leave Me to Myself and busy themselves with other things. Oh, how sad I am that souls do not recognize Love! (1385).

Oh, how painful it is to Me that souls so seldom unite themselves to Me in Holy Communion. I wait for souls, and they are indifferent toward Me. I love them tenderly and sincerely, and they distrust Me. I want to lavish My graces on them, and they do not want to accept them. They treat Me as a dead object, whereas My Heart is full of love and mercy (1447).

Holy Communion
in the life of Sister Faustina

The most solemn moment of my life is the moment when I receive Holy Communion. I long for each Holy Communion, and for every Holy Communion I give thanks to the Most Holy Trinity (1804).

Today, I prepare for the coming of the King.

What am I, and who are You, O Lord, King of eternal glory? O my heart, are you aware of who is coming to you today? Yes, I know, but–strangely–I am not able to grasp it. Oh, if He were just a king, but He is the King of kings, the Lord of lords. Before Him, all power and dominion tremble. He is coming to my heart today...

I hear Him approaching. I go out to meet Him and invite Him. When He entered the dwelling of my heart, it was filled with such reverence that it fainted with fear, falling at His feet. Jesus gives her His hand and graciously permits her to take her place beside Him. He reassures her saying, See, I have left My heavenly throne to become united with you. What you see is just a tiny part and already your soul swoons with love. How amazed will your heart be when you see Me in all My glory. But I want to tell you that eternal life must begin already here on earth through Holy Communion. Each Holy Communion makes you more capable of communing with God throughout eternity (1810).

THE CHAPLET
OF DIVINE MERCY

Jesus dictated the Chaplet of Divine Mercy to Sister Faustina in Vilnius in 1935. In the revelations that followed He disclosed to her its value and efficacy, as well as the promises He attached to it.

In this prayer we are offering the *Body and Blood, Soul and Divinity* of Jesus Christ to God the Father. We are uniting ourselves with His sacrifice offered on the Cross for the salvation of the world. By offering God the Father His *most dearly beloved Son,* we are using the most convincing argument with which to be heard. We are asking for mercy *for us and for the whole world.* The word "us" refers to the person reciting the chaplet and those for whom he desires to offer it or for whom he should pray. The "whole world" indicates all people living on earth and the souls in Purgatory. By praying the words of this chaplet we are performing an act of love toward our neighbor, which along with trust, is the indispensable condition for obtaining graces.

Jesus promised, *It pleases Me to grant everything they ask of Me by saying the chaplet* (1541) and He added, *if (it). . . be compatible with My will* (1731). The special promises pertain to the hour of death; that is, the grace of a happy and peaceful death. This grace may be obtained not only by those who recite the chaplet with confidence and perseverance but also by the dying, at whose bedside others will pray it. *Priests*, Jesus said, *will recommend it to sinners as their last hope of salvation. Even if there were a sinner most hardened, if he were to recite this chaplet only once, he would receive grace from My infinite mercy* (687). Jesus promised to grant grace to those who recite this prayer at least once in their lifetime, providing it is said with an attitude of complete trust, humility, and a sincere, deep sorrow for sin.

The Chaplet
of Divine Mercy
(on ordinary rosary beads)

Begin with:

Our Father, Who art in heaven, hallowed be Thy name; Thy kingdom come; Thy will be done on earth as it is in heaven. Give us this day our daily bread; and forgive us our trespasses as we forgive those who trespass against us; and lead us not into temptation, but deliver us from evil. Amen.

Hail Mary, full of grace. The Lord is with Thee. Blessed art Thou among women, and blessed is the fruit of Thy womb, Jesus. Holy Mary, Mother of God, pray for us sinners, now and at the hour of our death. Amen.

I believe in God, the Father almighty, creator of heaven and earth.

I believe in Jesus Christ, His only Son, our Lord. He was conceived by the power of the Holy Spirit, and born of the Virgin Mary. He suffered under Pontius Pilate, was crucified, died, and was buried. He descended to the dead. On the third day He rose again. He ascended into heaven, and is seated at the right hand of the Father. He will come again to judge the living and the dead.

I believe in the Holy Spirit, the holy Catholic Church, the communion of saints, the forgiveness of sins, the resurrection of the body, and the life everlasting. Amen.

On the large bead before each decade:

Eternal Father, I offer You the Body and Blood, Soul and Divinity of Your dearly beloved Son, Our Lord Jesus Christ, in atonement for our sins and those of the whole world.

On the 10 small beads of each decade:

For the sake of His sorrowful Passion, have mercy on us and on the whole world.

Conclude with: (after five decades)

Holy God, Holy Mighty One, Holy Immortal One, have mercy on us and on the whole world (3 times).

THE HOUR OF MERCY

As often as you hear the clock strike the third hour, immerse yourself completely in My mercy, adoring and glorifying it; invoke its omnipotence for the whole world, and particularly for poor sinners; for at that moment mercy was opened wide for every soul (1320).

It is Jesus' desire that the moment of His Death on the Cross (3:00 p.m.) be venerated every day; the hour which He said *was the hour of grace for the whole world—mercy triumphed over justice* (1572). At this hour, He wants us to meditate upon His sorrowful Passion because it reveals most distinctly the love God has for His people. At this time Jesus wants us to worship and glorify the Mercy of God, and, by the merits of His passion, to implore the necessary graces for ourselves and the whole world, especially for sinners.

Try your best, Jesus instructed Sister Faustina, *to make the Stations of the Cross in this hour, provided that your duties permit it; and if you are not able to make the Stations of the Cross, then at least step into the chapel for a moment and adore, in the Blessed*

Sacrament, My heart, which is full of mercy; and should you be unable to step into the chapel, immerse yourself in prayer there where you happen to be, if only for a very brief instant (1572).

This is the hour, as Jesus promised, in which *you can obtain everything for yourself and for others for the asking* (1572). *I will refuse nothing to the soul that makes a request of Me in virtue of My Passion* (1320).

The Hour of Mercy is associated explicitly with three o'clock in the afternoon. Our prayers at this time should be directed to Jesus, and our petitions should appeal to the merits of His sorrowful Passion.

Prayers at the Hour of Mercy

O Blood and Water, which gushed forth from the Heart of Jesus as a fount of Mercy for us, I trust in You (187).

***

You Yourself, Jesus, surely out of love for us, underwent such a terrible Passion. Your Father's justice would have been propitiated with a single sigh from You, and all Your self-abasement is solely the work of Your mercy and Your inconceivable love. . . . At the moment of Your death on the Cross, You bestowed upon us eternal life; allowing Your most holy side to be opened, You opened an inexhaustible spring of mercy for us, giving us Your dearest possession, the Blood and Water from Your Heart. Such is the omnipotence of Your mercy. From it all grace flows to us (1747).

***

O Jesus, eternal Truth, our Life, I call upon You and beg Your mercy for poor sinners. O sweetest Heart of my Lord, full of pity and unfathomable mercy, I plead with you for poor sinners. O Most Sacred Heart, Fount of Mercy from which gush forth rays of inconceivable graces upon the entire human race, I beg of You light for poor sinners. O Jesus, be mindful of Your own bitter Passion and do not permit the loss of souls redeemed at so dear a price of Your most precious Blood.

O Jesus, stretched out upon the cross, I implore You, give me the grace of doing faithfully the most holy will of Your Father, in all things, always and everywhere. And when this will of God will seem to me very harsh and difficult to fulfill, it is then I beg You, Jesus, may power and strength flow upon me from your wounds, and may my lips keep repeating, "Your will be done, O Lord."

O Savior of the world, Lover of man's salvation, who in such terrible torment and pain, forgot Yourself to think only of the salvation of souls, O most compassionate Jesus, grant me the grace to forget myself that I may live totally for souls, helping You in the work of salvation, according to the most holy will of Your Father (1265).

***

You expired, Jesus, but the source of life gushed forth for souls, and the ocean of mercy opened up for the whole world. O Fount of Life, unfathomable Divine Mercy, envelop the whole world and empty Yourself out upon us (1319).

SPREADING
THE DIVINE MERCY DEVOTION

Souls who spread the honor of My mercy I shield through their entire life as a tender mother her infant, and at the hour of death I will not be a Judge for them, but the Merciful Savior (1075). By these words, Jesus is encouraging us to spread the worship of Divine Mercy; He has promised maternal care to those who do so by shielding them throughout their entire life and at the hour of death. He made a singular promise to priests saying, *Hardened sinners will repent on hearing their words, when they will speak about My unfathomable mercy, about the compassion I have for them in My Heart. To priests who will proclaim and extol My mercy, I will give wondrous power, and I will annoint their words and touch the hearts of those to whom they will speak* (1521).

The foundation for the worship and apostolate of Divine Mercy is the testimony of one's own life according to the spirit of this devotion; namely, the spirit of childlike confidence in the goodness and omnipotence of God, accompanied by an active love of one's neighbor.

All those souls, Jesus said, *who will glorify My mercy and spread its worship, encouraging others to trust in My mercy, will not experience terror at the hour of death. My mercy will shield them in that final battle* (1540).

***

O Eternal Love, I want all the souls You have created to come to know You. I would like to be a priest, for then I would speak without cease about Your mercy to sinful souls drowned in despair. I would like to be a missionary and carry the light of faith to savage nations in order to make You known to souls, and to be completely consumed for them and to die a martyr's death by completely emptying myself and denying myself for love of You, O Jesus, and of immortal souls. Great love can change small things into great ones (302).

It is my greatest desire that souls should recognize You as their eternal happiness, that they should come to believe in Your goodness and glorify Your infinite mercy (305).

SELECTED PRAYERS
FROM SISTER FAUSTINA'S DIARY

The Praises of the Divine Mercy

The Love of God is the flower - Mercy the fruit. Let the doubting soul read these considerations on Divine Mercy and become trusting.

Divine Mercy, gushing forth from the bosom of the Father, I trust in You.

Divine Mercy, greatest attribute of God,
I trust in You.

Divine Mercy, incomprehensible mystery,
I trust in You.

Divine Mercy, fount gushing forth from the mystery of the Most Blessed Trinity,
I trust in You.

Divine Mercy, unfathomed by any intellect, human or angelic, I trust in You.

Divine Mercy, from which wells forth all life and happiness, I trust in You.

Divine Mercy, better than the heavens,
   I trust in You.
Divine Mercy, source of miracles and wonders,
   I trust in You.
Divine Mercy, encompassing the whole universe,
   I trust in You.
Divine Mercy, descending to earth in the Person
   of the Incarnate Word, I trust in You.
Divine Mercy, which flowed out from the open
   wound of the Heart of Jesus, I trust in You.
Divine Mercy, enclosed in the Heart of Jesus for
   us, and especially for sinners, I trust in You.
Divine Mercy, unfathomed in the institution of
   the Sacred Host, I trust in You.
Divine Mercy, in the founding of Holy Church,
   I trust in You.
Divine Mercy, in the Sacrament of Holy Baptism,
   I trust in You.
Divine Mercy, in our justification through Jesus
   Christ, I trust in You.
Divine Mercy, accompanying us through our
   whole life, I trust in You.
Divine Mercy, embracing us especially at the
   hour of death, I trust in You.

Divine Mercy, endowing us with immortal life,
I trust in You.

Divine Mercy, accompanying us at every
moment of our life, I trust in You.

Divine Mercy, shielding us from the fire of hell,
I trust in You.

Divine Mercy, in the conversion of hardened
sinners, I trust in You.

Divine Mercy, astonishment for Angels,
incomprehensible to Saints, I trust in You.

Divine Mercy, unfathomed in all the mysteries
of God, I trust in You.

Divine Mercy, lifting us out of every misery,
I trust in You.

Divine Mercy, source of our happiness and joy,
I trust in You.

Divine Mercy, in calling us forth from
nothingness to existence, I trust in You.

Divine Mercy, embracing all the works
of His hands, I trust in You.

Divine Mercy, crown of all of God's handiwork,
I trust in You.

Divine Mercy, in which we are all immersed,
I trust in You.

Divine Mercy, sweet relief for anguished hearts,
   I trust in You.
Divine Mercy, only hope of despairing souls,
   I trust in You.
Divine Mercy, repose of hearts, peace amidst
   fear, I trust in You.
Divine Mercy, delight and ecstasy of holy souls,
   I trust in You.
Divine Mercy, inspiring hope against all hope,
   I trust in You (949).

   Eternal God, in whom mercy is endless and
the treasury of compassion inexhaustible, look
kindly upon us and increase Your mercy in us,
that in difficult moments we might not despair
nor become despondent, but with great confidence submit ourselves to Your holy will,
which is Love and Mercy itself (950).

   O incomprehensible and limitless Mercy
Divine, to extol and adore You worthily, who
can? Supreme attribute of Almighty God, You
are the sweet hope for sinful man (951).

Before the Blessed Sacrament

I adore You, Lord and Creator, hidden in the Blessed Sacrament. I adore You for all the works of Your hands, that reveal to me so much wisdom, goodness and mercy, O Lord. You have spread so much beauty over the earth, and it tells me about Your beauty, even though these beautiful things are but a faint reflection of You, Incomprehensible Beauty. And although You have hidden Yourself and concealed Your beauty, my eye, enlightened by faith, reaches You, and my soul recognizes its Creator, its Highest Good; and my heart is completely immersed in prayer of adoration.

My Lord and Creator, Your goodness encourages me to converse with You. Your mercy abolishes the chasm which separates the Creator from the creature. To converse with You, O Lord, is the delight of my heart. In You I find everything that my heart could desire. Here Your light illumines my mind, enabling it to know You more and more deeply. Here streams of graces flow down upon my heart. Here my soul draws eternal life.

O my Lord and Creator, You alone, beyond all these gifts, give Your own self to me and unite Yourself intimately with Your miserable creature. Here, without searching for words, our hearts understand each other. Here, no one is able to interrupt our conversation. What I talk to You about, Jesus, is our secret, which creatures shall not know.... These are secret acts of forgiveness, known only to Jesus and me; this is the mystery of His mercy, which embraces each soul separately. For this incomprehensible goodness of Yours, I adore You, O Lord and Creator, with all my heart and all my soul. And, although my worship is so little and poor, I am at peace because I know that You know it is sincere, however inadequate... (1692).

In Thanksgiving

O Jesus, eternal God, thank You for Your countless graces and blessings. Let every beat of my heart be a new hymn of thanksgiving to You, O God. Let every drop of my blood circulate for You, Lord. My soul is one hymn in adoration of Your mercy. I love You, God, for Yourself alone (1794).

For Divine Mercy for the World

O Greatly Merciful God, Infinite Goodness, today all mankind calls out from the abyss of its misery to Your mercy–to Your compassion, O God; and it is with its mighty voice of misery that it cries out. Gracious God, do not reject the prayer of this earth's exiles! O Lord, Goodness beyond our understanding, Who are acquainted with our misery through and through, and know that by our own power we cannot ascend to You, we implore You: anticipate us with Your grace and keep on increasing Your mercy is us, that we may faithfully do Your holy will all through our life and at death's hour. Let the omnipotence of Your mercy shield us from the darts of our salvation's enemies, that we may with confidence, as Your children, await Your final coming–that day known to You alone. And we expect to obtain everything promised us by Jesus in spite of all our wretchedness. For Jesus is our hope: Through His merciful Heart, as through an open gate, we pass through to heaven (1570).

For the Holy Church and Priests

O my Jesus, I beg You on behalf of the whole Church: Grant [her] love and the light of Your Spirit, and give power to the words of priests so that hardened hearts might be brought to repentance and return to You, O Lord. Lord, give us holy priests; You yourself maintain them in holiness. O Divine and Great High Priest, may the power of Your mercy accompany them everywhere and protect them from the devil's traps and snares which are continually being set for the souls of priests. May the power of Your mercy, O Lord, shatter and bring to naught all that might tarnish the sanctity of priests, for You can do all things (1052).

Jesus, my most beloved, I beg You for the triumph of the Church, for blessings on the Holy Father, and on all the clergy; for the grace of conversion for impenitent sinners. And I ask You for a special blessing and for light, O Jesus, for the priests before whom I will make my confessions throughout my lifetime (240).

For One's Country

Most merciful Jesus, I beseech You through the intercession of Your Saints, and especially the intercession of Your dearest Mother who nurtured You from childhood, bless my native land. I beg You, Jesus, look not on our sins, but on the tears of little children, on the hunger and cold they suffer. Jesus, for the sake of these innocent ones, grant me the grace that I am asking of You for my country (286).

To Obtain Love of God

Most sweet Jesus, set on fire my Love for You and transform me into Yourself. Divinize me that my deeds may be pleasing to You. May this be accomplished by the power of the Holy Communion which I receive daily (1289).

To Obtain an Understanding of God

I often ask the Lord Jesus for an intellect enlightened by faith. I express this to the Lord in these words: Jesus, give me an intellect, a great intellect, for this only, that I may understand You better; because the better I get to know You, the more ardently will I love You. Jesus, I ask You for a powerful intellect, that I may understand divine and lofty matters. Jesus, give me a keen intellect with which I will get to know Your Divine Essence and Your indwelling, Triune life. Give my intellect these capacities and aptitudes by means of

Your special grace. Although I know that there is a capability through grace which the Church gives me, there is still a treasure of graces which You give us, O Lord, when we ask You for them. But if my request is not pleasing to You, then I beg You, do not give me the inclination to pray thus (1474).

Invocations of Trust

O my God, my only hope, I have placed all my trust in You, and I know I shall not be disappointed (317).

***

I know the full power of Your mercy, and I trust that You will give me everything Your feeble child needs (898).

***

O Jesus, concealed in the Blessed Sacrament of the Altar, my only love and mercy, I commend to You all the needs of my body and soul. You can help me, because You are Mercy itself. In You lies all my hope (1751).

Prayer of Trust

I fly to Your mercy, Compassionate God, who alone are good. Although my misery is great, and my offenses are many, I trust in Your mercy, because You are the God of mercy; and, from time immemorial, it has never been heard of, nor do heaven or earth remember, that a soul trusting in Your mercy has been disappointed.

O God of compassion, You alone can justify me, and You will never reject me when I, contrite, approach Your merciful Heart, where no one has ever been refused, even if he were the greatest sinner (1730).

For the Grace to be Merciful to Others

I want to be completely transformed into Your Mercy and to be Your living reflection, O Lord. May the greatest of all divine attributes, that of Your unfathomable mercy, pass through my heart and soul to my neighbor.

Help me, O Lord, that my eyes may be merciful, so that I may never suspect or judge from appearances, but look for what is beautiful in my neighbors' souls and come to their rescue.

Help me, that my ears may be merciful, so that I may give heed to my neighbors' needs and not be indifferent to their pains and moanings.

Help me, O Lord, that my tongue may be merciful, so that I should never speak negatively of my neighbor, but have a word of comfort and forgiveness for all.

Help me, O Lord, that my hands may be merciful and filled with good deeds, so that I may do only good to my neighbors and take upon myself the more difficult and toilsome tasks.

Help me, that my feet may be merciful, so that I may hurry to assist my neighbor, overcoming my own fatigue and weariness. My true rest is in the service of my neighbor.

Help me, O Lord, that my heart may be merciful so that I myself may feel all the sufferings of my neighbor. I will refuse my heart to no one, I will be sincere even with those who, I know, will abuse my kindness. And I will lock myself up in the most merciful Heart of Jesus. I will bear my own suffering in silence. May Your Mercy, O Lord, rest upon me (163).

For the Conversion of Sinners

God of great mercy, who deigned to send us Your only-begotten Son as the greatest proof of Your fathomless love and mercy, You do not reject sinners; but in Your boundless mercy You have opened for them also Your treasures, treasures from which they can draw abundantly, not only justification, but also all the sanctity that a soul can attain. Father of great mercy, I desire that all hearts turn with confidence to Your infinite mercy. No one will be justified before You if he is not accompanied by

Your unfathomable mercy. When You reveal the mystery of Your mercy to us, there will not be enough of eternity to properly thank You for it (1122).

***

O Jesus, how sorry I feel for poor sinners. Jesus, grant them contrition and repentance. Remember Your own sorrowful Passion. I know Your infinite mercy and cannot bear it that a soul that has cost You so much should perish. Jesus, give me the souls of sinners; let Your mercy rest upon them. Take everything away from me, but give me souls. I want to become a sacrificial host for sinners. Let the shell of my body conceal my offering, for Your Most Sacred Heart is also hidden in a Host, and certainly You are a living sacrifice. Transform me into Yourself, O Jesus, that I may be a living sacrifice and pleasing to You. I desire to atone at each moment for poor sinners. . . O my Creator and Father of great mercy, I trust in You, for You are Goodness Itself (908).

In Times of Suffering

O Living Host, support me in this exile, that I may be empowered to walk faithfully in the footsteps of the Savior. I do not ask, Lord, that You take me down from the cross, but I implore You to give me the strength to remain steadfast upon it. I want to be stretched out upon the cross as You were, Jesus. I want all the tortures and pains that You suffered. I want to drink the cup of bitterness to the dregs (1484).

***

O my Jesus, give me strength to endure suffering so that I may not make a wry face when I drink the cup of bitterness. Help me Yourself to make my sacrifice pleasing to You. May it not be tainted by my self-love. . . may everything that is in me, both my misery and my strength, give praise to You, O Lord (1740).

For a Happy Death

O merciful Jesus, stretched on the cross, be mindful of the hour of our death. O most merciful Heart of Jesus, opened with a lance, shelter me at the last moment of my life. O Blood and Water, which gushed forth from the Heart of Jesus as a fount of unfathomable mercy for me (cleanse me of my sins and offences). O dying Jesus, Hostage of mercy, avert the Divine wrath at the hour of my death (813).

***

O my Jesus, may the last days of my exile be spent totally according to Your most holy will. I unite my sufferings, my bitterness and my last agony itself to Your Sacred Passion; and I offer myself for the whole world to implore an abundance of God's mercy for souls, and in particular for the souls (of sinners). I firmly trust and commit myself entirely to Your holy will, which is mercy itself. Your mercy will be everything for me at the last hour (1574).

To the Mother of God

O Mary, my Mother and my Lady, I offer You my soul, my body, my life and my death, and all that will follow it. I place everything in Your hands. O my Mother, cover my soul with Your virginal mantle and grant me the grace of purity of heart, soul and body. Defend me with Your power against all enemies. . . O lovely lily! You are for me a mirror, O my Mother! (79)

***

Mother of God, Your soul was plunged into a sea of bitterness; look upon Your child and teach it to suffer and to love while suffering. Fortify my soul that pain will not break it. Mother of grace, teach me to live by (the power of) God (315).

***

O sweet Mother of God, I model my life on You; You are for me the bright dawn; in

You I lose myself, enraptured. O Mother, Immaculate Virgin, in You the divine ray is reflected, midst storms, 'tis You who teach me to love the Lord, O my shield and defense from the foe (1232).

PRAYER TO OBTAIN GRACES through the intercession of Saint Faustina

O Jesus, who filled Saint Faustina with profound veneration for Your boundless Mercy, deign, if it be Your holy will, to grant me, through her intercession, the grace for which I fervently pray...

My sins render me unworthy of Your Mercy, but be mindful of Sister Faustina's spirit of sacrifice and self-denial, and reward her virtue by granting the petition which, with childlike trust, I present to You through her intercession.

Our Father..., Hail Mary..., Glory...
Saint Faustina, pray for us.

Whoever receives a grace through the intercession
of Saint Faustina is asked to write to:

The Congregation of the Sisters of Our Lady of Mercy
ul. Siostry Faustyny 3/9
30-420 Kraków
Poland.

Pauline
BOOKS & MEDIA

The Daughters of St. Paul operate book and media centers at the following addresses. Visit, call or write the one nearest you today, or find us on the World Wide Web, www.pauline.org

CALIFORNIA
3908 Sepulveda Blvd, Culver City, CA
  90230 310-397-8676
5945 Balboa Avenue, San Diego, CA
  92111 858-565-9181
46 Geary Street, San Francisco, CA
  94108 415-781-5180

FLORIDA
145 S.W. 107th Avenue, Miami, FL
  33174 305-559-6715

HAWAII
1143 Bishop Street, Honolulu, HI
  96813 808-521-2731
Neighbor Islands call:
  800-259-8463

ILLINOIS
172 North Michigan Avenue, Chicago,
  IL 60601 312-346-4228

LOUISIANA
4403 Veterans Memorial Blvd,
  Metairie, LA 70006 504-887-7631

MASSACHUSETTS
Rte. 1, 885 Providence Hwy, Dedham,
  MA 02026 781-326-5385

MISSOURI
9804 Watson Road, St. Louis, MO
  63126 314-965-3512

NEW JERSEY
561 U.S. Route 1, Wick Plaza,
  Edison, NJ 08817 732-572-1200

NEW YORK
150 East 52nd Street, New York, NY
  10022 212-754-1110
78 Fort Place, Staten Island, NY
  10301 718-447-5071

OHIO
2105 Ontario Street, Cleveland, OH
  44115 216-621-9427

PENNSYLVANIA
9171-A Roosevelt Blvd, Philadelphia,
  PA 19114 215-676-9494

SOUTH CAROLINA
243 King Street, Charleston, SC
  29401 843-577-0175

TENNESSEE
4811 Poplar Avenue, Memphis, TN
  38117 901-761-2987

TEXAS
114 Main Plaza, San Antonio, TX
  78205 210-224-8101

VIRGINIA
1025 King Street, Alexandria, VA
  22314 703-549-3806

CANADA
3022 Dufferin Street, Toronto,
  Ontario, Canada M6B 3T5
  416-781-9131
1155 Yonge Street, Toronto,
  Ontario, Canada M4T 1W2
  416-934-3440

¡También somos su fuente para libros, videos y música en español!

The Congregation
of the Sisters
# of Our Lady of Mercy

to which Saint Faustina belonged, is dedicated, in collaboration with the infinite mercy of God, to the task of saving souls. Special care is directed toward girls and women in need of moral assistance. It also carries out Saint Faustina's mission by proclaiming the message Jesus entrusted to her and by imploring God's mercy for the whole world.

Novitiate
ul. Siostry Faustyny 3/9
30-420 Kraków, Poland

Generalate
ul. Żytnia 3/9
01-014 Warszawa, Poland

United States Address
Sisters of Our Lady of Mercy
241 Neponset Avenue
Dorchester, MA 02122